RITA ANN HIGGINS

Philomena's Revenge

SALMON POETRY

First published in 1992 by
Salmon Publishing, Galway.

This edition 1993 by
Salmon Publishing Ltd
A division of Poolbeg Enterprises Ltd,
Knocksedan House,
Swords, Co. Dublin, Ireland

**Salmon Publishing Ltd receives financial assistance from
The Arts Council/An Chomhairle Ealaíon**

A catalogue record for this book is available from the British Library.

ISBN 1 897648 10 3

Cover photograph by Gillian Buckley
Cover Design by Poolbeg Group Services Ltd
Set by Mac Book Limited
Printed by The Guernsey Press Limited,
Vale, Guernsey, Channel Islands.

Acknowledgements are due to the following anthologies in which some of these poems first appeared:

The New Younger Irish Poets (Blackstaff); *Wildish Things* (Attic); *Living Landscape* (Cork); *Sleeping with Monsters* (Wolfhound),

and the following journals and newspapers:

Cyphers; The Salmon; The Honest Ulsterman; Stet; Phoebe (USA); The Irish Reporter; New York Newsday; Irish Echo (New York); Writing in the West (The Connacht Tribune); The Galway Advertiser.

Several of these poems have been broadcast on RTE Radio 1 & 2, and on BBC Radio 4.

Contents

Do m'athair

They Believe in Clint Eastwood

In Cork prison
on Ash Wednesday
the warders have
black crosses painted
where the Cyclops
had his eye.

They believe in
the Trinity,

They believe in
reincarnation,

They believe in
dust and ashes,

They believe in
Jesus with long hair,

They believe in
Clint Eastwood,

They believe in
key consortium;

They believe in
the letter of the law.

God Dodgers Anonymous

The Jehovah Witness
asked her
if she had a God.

No beating
around the burning bush
for this lassie.
Straight from the hip,
eyeball to eyeball job.

Have you a God?

It depends
on how you look at it,
I haven't a pot to spew libations in
yet the Gods are hopping up
all over the joint,

and funny thing
it's never
with chalice and host,
it's always
with book and pen;
sometimes a sugary grin.

'I'm God
give us four pounds
or I'll kick
your shite in.'

The Witness
witnessing a new line
in idolatry,
was flummoxed.

She told the one
who was beyond saving
to have a nice day
(she said it twice for effect.)

I will, she assured,
I'll have a bastarding ball
dodging the Gods
round the grand piano
that isn't really there at all,

spitting fire
awaiting the second coming,
and when I'm not fasting for fun
I can always spend an hour or two

chewing the Moroccan sturdite binding
off the book of Daniel
and before you can say
'Watch out for the Watchtower,'

I'll see the three horsemen of the Apocalypse
(the fourth is having a hip operation)
strutting in here, proffering
gold, frankincense and more.

Every Second Sunday

'Can't talk now
I'm rushing up
to pay the raffle,

"The Cashel Circle"

I owe two weeks.

If I won
that hundred
no bill-boy
would get a shaggin' penny
that's for sure.

I'd buy myself
two pairs of shoes,
shop shoes,
I'd wear them

every second Sunday.'

Him and His Terrier

The demons
made his fists dance,
no lamppost was safe.

Before this
he was fussy about
who he said hello to.
No Eastsider would ever get
his greeting.

All his stories had
Atlantic Ocean connections;
a sailor in his heart
but he never left town.

They sought him out
for his good conversation,
it was water water everywhere.

He got worse
the stories got better
more sea, less land.
He went further away
still he never left town.

They say his brain
got sizzled with the booze.
Methylated Spirits in the end,
it stole his conversation
no more fights with lampposts.

Not fussy about Eastsiders now,
his words are few, but he repeats them.
Hello to everyone from the corner,
him and his terrier.

Hurricane in a Tea Cup

She had problems
with tittle tattle,
she turned everything into
a hurricane in a tea cup.

When Evvy Murray
told her mother
'Does she ever do anything
but push that pram
and do the lotto?'

She got very upset,
said her clock was haywire
and whose business was it anyway

if she walked round
in the middle of the night
with a pram full of briquettes.
They were her briquettes,
finders keepers,

more in that one's line
get a man first
much less try keeping
him warm.

She went on for weeks
hashing and rehashing
what Evvy Murray said.

The briquette-finding affair
and all pram-pushing stories
took a sudden end
the time she threw her biological clock
out the window;

Evvy Murray's cat
had nine glorious lives
it was his turn to lotto
and he lost.

Reading

To a group of prisoners
in a locked room
with a cage at the back.
It housed a warder
who lay across two chairs.

When he got restless
or peckish
he pranced up and down
in his new shoes
(they were always new
because they rarely touched ground).

'Slouched warder hears poetry
in horizontal position.'

A volunteer
made me tea,
chocolate biscuits
offered.

I read,
they listened
the one in the cage yawned
an uninterested-in-poetry yawn
(I know an uninterested-in-poetry yawn
a mile off; I interpret them).

I read some more,
a volley of questions,
some comments,
explosive laughter escaped
time and time again.

Their hunger for knowledge
stalked between lines of poems,
behind falling vowels,
in and out of hooks of question marks
under jaded asterisks;
they wanted to know
they wanted to know.

Seconds galloped all over us
minutes ricocheted
two hours shot by,
we were all casualties.

With the jingle of keys
I was free to go
handshakes, smiles
much left unsaid,

the distance between us
several poems shorter.

I feared the man in the cage.

Philomena's Revenge

As a teenager
she was like any other,
boys, the craic,
smoking down the backs.

Later there was talk
she broke things,
furniture and glass,
her mother's heart.

'Mad at the world,'
the old women nod
round each other's faces.

But it was more
than that
and for less
she was punished.

That weekend
she didn't leave a cup alone
every chair hit the wall,
Philomena's revenge.

Soon after
she was shifted
and given the shocks.

Round each other's faces
the old women nod,
'Treatment, treatment
they've given her the treatment.'

These days
she gets on with the furniture,
wears someone else's walk,
sees visions in glass.

She's good too
for getting the messages;
small things, bread and milk
sometimes the paper,

and closing the gate
after her father drives out,
she waits for his signal
he always shouts twice,

'Get the gate Philo,
get the gate, girl.'

People Who Wear Cardigans
   ## Are Subversive

People who wear cardigans
are the type of people
who say,

'Would you get us
the Gold Flake
out of the cardi in the hall stand
before the race starts
like a good girl.'

People who wear cardigans are subversive.

I know a man who swore
'All popes are good.'
He was a C wearer.

They are more likely
to call their children strange names.
I knew one with a sly neck
who had a habit of saying
out of the corner of his mouth,
'J.C.B. Kellogg and Dry Bread
your tea is ready.'
He was a seven day a week C wearer.

They keep their money
and bits of granny
in biscuit tins

under the stairs.
They pray for rain
and the postponement of Christmas,
plus the evacuation of all children
to the plural of Pluto.

People who wear cardigans are subversive.

They harbour resentments against
slickless phones.
I knew a heavy breather once,
when leaving the scene
he said into the smutty night air,

'Here I am,
full of ooohs and aaahs
and the phone is jammed.'
He was a two a day C wearer.

Other C wearers
wear socks with sandals,
it goes with the territory,
'Keep the lungs
and the soles of the feet hot
and the rest will take care of itself,'
a C wearer's motto.

They get up before themselves,
get down before no one,
never shoot themselves in the foot,

but in caution
keep all loose legs under the table.

People who wear cardigans are subversive.

They wear them to hide things,
like biscuit tins,
granny bits,
rain storms,
lost Christmases,
protruding calendars,
and deep resentments.

People who wear cardigans are subversive.

Born agains and born liars
the lot of them.
One swears his grandfather could do a wheelie
while a suppressed piano
wavered on his altered ego,
he was a C wearer.

Cravat merchants
with skull rings at the gullet,
devil worshippers,
Claddagh ringers,
duffle coaters, bin lidders,

People who wear cardigans are subversive.

Misogynist

Is the boss in?
Could he give us
a yard of a tow,

the engine's after
collapsin' on me again,
she is, the bitch.

The Deserter

He couldn't wait
just up and died
on me.

Two hours,
two hours
I spent ironing
them shirts
and he didn't even
give me the pleasure
of dirtying them,

that's the type
of person he was,
would rather die
than please you.

But in his favour
I will say this for him,
he made a lovely corpse.
Looked better dead
than he did in our front room
before the telly,

right cock-of-the-walk
in that coffin,
head slightly tilted back
like he was going to say
'My dear people.'

He couldn't wait,
never,
like the time
before the All-Ireland
we were going to Mass,

he had to have a pint
or he'd have the gawks, he said.
That's the type he was,
talk dirty in front of any woman.

No stopping him
when he got that ulcer out,
but where did it get him,

wax-faced above
in the morgue
that's where.

He's not giving
out to me now
for using Jeyes Fluid
on the kitchen floor,

or stuffing the cushions
with his jaded socks. . . .
and what jaded them?
Pub crawling jaded them,
that's what.

He's tight-lipped now
about my toe separators,
before this
he would threaten them
on the hot ash.

The next time
I spend two hours
ironing shirts for him
he'll wear them.

Questionnaire After Leaving
Aillwee Cave

Does your dog bite?
(land owner, working class,
jumped-up third generation
guttersnipe or other)

How many full stops in The Gulag Archipelago?

Do you wear coloured condoms?
(green, purple, gold, black or other)

Do you think Boris Yeltsin and Teresa of the Little
Flower are the same person?

Do you wear two at a time?

Do you see the humour in unemployment?

Do you believe Elvis is still alive?

Should we have free coal?

Did you have dark thoughts in the cave?

What colour should it be?

Spell Acetylsalicylic acid.

Does your wife beat you?
(yes, no, not sure)

Did you ever have impure thoughts about cheese?

Do you ride buses?

About Bree, I see mmmmmmm.
Do you believe in the power of the reflexologist?

Do all Roses of Tralee who don't make it
join the I.R.A.?

Does it hurt . . . no, no this is the bus question, wake up.

Do you give good phone?

Does your car own you?

Does your Credit Union own you?

Did you want to reach out
and touch someone in the cave?

Was it God?

Good.

Four Steps Nowhere

In Limerick jail
a woman is guarded
in the yard.

For every step she takes
the two guards guarding her
take four.

Even if the guards
went to the pictures
or to bingo,
the guarded one
wasn't going home
for tea, rashers
and fried bread.

The fence round the yard
passes our celestial bodies
souls going to heaven
and planets not yet dreamt of.

Light of the Moon

Question:
Can you tell me
the way to the maternity?

Answer:
Walk on a beach
in the West of Ireland
at four in the morning
in the middle of summer
with a man who's six foot two
and you'll get there
sooner or later.

Question:
Is his height the problem?

Answer:
No, the problem rises   (fallic)
when you stop
to look at the moon.

Question:
So is the moon
the problem?

Answer:
No, not the moon itself
but the glare from the moon
which makes you say

n seagull Russian,
'Fuse me bix foot skew
in your stocking wheat
bould you kind werribly
if I jay on the bat of my flack
for the bext three quarters of a bour
the boon is milling me.'

Question:
And that's the answer?

Answer:
No, that's the question.
When he lies on top of you
for the next three quarters of an hour
shielding you from the light of the moon
the answer comes to you.

Question:
Like a flash?

Answer.
No, like the thundering tide.

Crooked Smiles

for B.A.

'What good is having
framed family portraits
hanging on your wall?

Better if your kids
are running round
in ventilated shoes
but happy,

than sitting still
looking out at you
from a framed lie.

The lie is not the children
but the one there
with the crooked smile.

The force of his fist
made my smile crooked a few times
but I got over it.

Better to have your own teeth
and the chance of a good neighbour's
half bowl of anything,

than a sour blooded low-life
who makes framed pictures
hang side-ways on your wall.'

Way to Go

Decent people
drift off in their sleep
quietly and without fuss.

Others, less considerate
choose middle of the night
or lunchtimes,
(anything for notice).

The adventurous
break their necks
on the Alps.

They could try
falling down
the stairs at home
and get the same result,
a great saving on plane tickets,
hotel accommodation, etc.

Others love clatter,
it's the supermarket for them,
can-falling-affair,
something like that;
out-with-a-bang merchants.

The courageous stand up to
iron horses, that's not funny
only very painful, one imagines.

Then there's the reckless
who go to Boston,
climb the John Hancock Tower,
the heart can't stand it.
They come home in a box
with their hands in their pockets.

As for me, proper coward,
give me priest prayers
and all buckshee indulgences.

If at all possible
let the priest be handsome
with warm hands
and entertaining breath.

Cloud Talker

Two men
are putting a roof
on the neighbour's shed.

They are both tall
very tall,
they look alike
very alike,
they would pass for brothers,
they would pass.

One hardly acknowledges her
(in fact for no bad reason
they don't anything each other).

The other one makes cloud talk.

She spies on them
from behind the net curtain
where she flushes out
stale and ancient tea-leaf schemes
from two breakfast cups.

This day without charity,
when she is pegging down
their aggressive sheets,
she says to cloud talker,

'I love a man
as tall as you,
as fair as you,
as blue-eyed as you,
but I can't put my hands
inside his shirt
because he's doing life.'

Just then
no-bad-reason spoke.
'Twin brother,' he said,
'enough of your talk,
you'll bring on the rain.
Throw me that hammer,
let's get on with the nails.

We've already been here
half a lifetime.'

Old Timers

She loves the clockman;
she leans on his shoulder
from her bicycle,
cycling slowly
through a field.

Slightly out of step,
the botched hip job
leaves him
one foot shorter
than the other.

She adores him;
his slight tick-over
his offbeat with time
but never with her heart.

Children have worn a path
for these older lovers,
harmony; not always seen,
the eye is good
but the heart is better.

They're heading for the pub now.
She loves the clockman;
she leans on his shoulder
from her bicycle.

On their return,
his short step less noticeable,
harmony more visible
as the falling together starts.

The treasured bicycle
now takes third place;
it trails like an unwanted relative,
uncle somebody.

When they hit home
he'll make the tea,
he'll rub her old feet,
they'll make yes and no sentences
for ages with love,

and if the voice is good
she'll sing out to her clockman
sweet youthful melodies,

making him forget
years, months, days,
minutes, seconds,
ticks, tocks,

until the only down-to-earth sound
is the click of her new teeth
as she whispers, gently,

'Love, oh love,
there's no time like the present.'

Waiting

The postman
grew tired,
the distance
stamped on his face,
the walk
was too much
for him

your letters
stopped coming.

His Shoulder Blades and Rome

for Pat Arthurs

The prisoner
in one of the cells
on the 4's landing
just under the roof,

can hear the soldiers
jumping up and down
trying to keep warm.

The prisoner
lying back in his bed
is thinking about
his ex-wife Maria,
(once the sunshine of his life),

about the time
he took her on holiday
to the Costa del Sol,
and how they separated
two weeks later.

It's getting colder,
colder than cold.
The soldiers are jumping
non-stop now;
they are freezing.

·33·

They are interrupting
his thoughts
about Maria, his ex-wife
(once the sunshine),

about the time
he took her on holidays to the Costa,

where she blew non-stop kisses
between his shoulder blades and Rome
easing the sting of yesterday's sun.

Butter Balls

Mountains of butter voucher recipients
met outside the meat hall
in Mill Street,
to hear misery guts
most miserable minister of miseries
spill the mean beans
about the extension
of the butter voucher scheme.

Oh mean miserable minister
misser of minor misdemeanours
and moving trains,
side tracker,
dirty talker,
spiller of misery,
and mean beans,
extender of butter voucher schemes,
tell us the miserable news.

'Good morning mealies,
it gives me great pleasure
(butter pleasure)
to tell all of you
who met today
outside the meat hall
in Mill Street,
which I nearly missed
owing to a minor misdemeanour,

that I oh miserablist of miseries
have made a meanagerial decision
for your benefit,
I've decided to extend
the butter voucher scheme
for another two years,

N.B. P.S. and etcetera.
It gives me minister of most miseries
ever more pleasure
(butter pleasure)
to tell you recipients
of unsocial smellfare,

that the above mentioned
butter voucher or B.V.
as we say at the MTs
has been increased from
54p to 55p per V.'

Dead Dogs and Nations

for Anne Kennedy

Other things upset her most
like dead dogs and nations.
Take the Gulf War,
she cried for every side,
it took her over
completely and without mercy.

Night, noon
and every phone call
she was Gulf grieving.

Once at a bus stop
she was overheard saying,
'They're killing my people.'

Her compassion immense;
her heart broke for
dead dogs and nations.

Her family
she cut out
at the greeting card stage,
one happy birthday to you
too many in a long line
of smiling faces
turned her off
she disowned the lot,
right down to the cooing babies

in Matinee coats and white souls.
These baby beauties
who brought out the best in others
did nothing for her.

Once she said out loud,
'Purgatory O Purgatory'
no one knew what she meant.

She didn't believe in innocence
or the power of prayer,
Popes and politicians could sizzle.

She went on caring
for dead dogs and other nations
she over-cared, she over-loved
but not really;

her own backyard
was a dark balloon
full of snakes and razor blades.

It's not that the grass
was always greener,
just it was always
under someone else's foot.

When Kelly's dog died
she broke for good.

I'll Have to Stop Thinking about Sex

for Tadgh Foley

People
are beginning
to notice.

Take
the two wans
at the market,
the fish market.

They looked
at each other
then they looked
at me.

Then
one said
to the other,

'Other,
that woman
is holding the French loaf
like it was a fisherman.'

They thought
that I thought
that the French loaf
was a you know what.

But they were wrong
'You know whats'
are often hard to fathom,

fishermen are fishermen
(spongy as earlobes).

The French loaf
was fresh and hot,

the only way
to hold it,
a reasonable way
to cool it.

They were wrong
the two wans,
with their know-your-loaf
philosophies
their all-seeing eyes
their all-fish tales.

Between Them

You only see
good-looking couples
out driving
on a Sunday afternoon.

His hair is blonde,
her eyes are blue.

Between them
they have no broken veins
stretch marks
Guinness guts
fat necks
barrel chests
or swollen ankles.

Between them
they never curse.
His give-away sign
is the way he holds the steering wheel
in the twenty-to-two position.

Her give-away sign
is the sweep of the perfume
she leaves lingering at the traffic lights
where the pedestrians often turn green.

Between them
they never eat fries
red or brown sauce
shanks of anybody
mackerel from the basin.
Putrid, they say, putrid.

Between them
they have no cholesterol in the blood
no coal in the shed,
everything is centrally heated,
it's easier that way
cuts out the middle man
and the mess.
Sometimes
when they are not out
looking good-looking,

between them
you could fit:
two McInerney Homes
three Berlin Walls
Martha Glynn's fantasies
four empty factories (I.D.A.)
seventeen rocket couriers (slightly overweight)
forty-eight good quality reconditioned colour T.V.s
incalculable curriculum Vs

cat fights
frog fights
bull fights
dog fights
broken hearts
hearts in jars
lost wars
lost teeth
teeth in jars
Pope's intentions
sexist free Bibles
Ceaucescu's wealth
Bush's blushes
tea-leaf prophecy classes
sole-of-the-feet prophecy classes
black-eye prophecy classes
white-of-the-eye prophecy classes
moveable feasts
grow your own cameras
poster poems
dirty water
and murder mysteries.

He Leaves the Ironing Board Open

He likes
crisp white shirts
and Tracy Chapman.
He leaves
the ironing board open
in his mobile home
near the motorway,
so that he is halfway there
if he ever makes the decision
to go out.

He plays
Tracy Chapman
really loud
in his mobile home
near the motorway,
so that he can't hear
the noise of the cars
or the screech of his loneliness
crashing into him
from every side.

Name Calling

In Loughan House
the warders prefer
to be called officers
but the inmates
call them screws.

There are no uniforms,
only the warders
who prefer to be called officers,
dress in unison
white shirt/black slacks.

The inmates
known to warders,
who prefer to be called officers,
as prisoners
in turn call them
penguins with a difference
who like to be called officers
who are always called screws.

The authorities say
detention centre,
the inmates say prison
they also say any news
screws, screws.

In Loughan House
the inmates
known to officers
who are nearly always
known as screws but sometimes
as penguins with a difference
are called for dinner
as prisoners,

they are called for letters
by their betters
they are called for tea.

In Loughan House
to some detention centre
to others pokey
where penguins with a difference
who want to be called officers
are nearly always called screws,

the inmates are called. . . .

A Time for Praise

She said
she never slept
with that hip,
and she knew everything
that went on
on the street,

and no use anyone saying
it was one of her crowd
robbed that car
when she knew full well
it was one of them neucks
from the hill,

didn't she see him
with her own eyes
and she a full six months
without a wink.

When she died,
with that hip,
the men made a tent
with white sheets
at her doorstep.

Carried out
through this tunnel of a tent,
she was placed
in the coffin,

the women keened.
Earlier when the news broke
her sisters asked for a lift
to Penney's to get the black gear.

'We'll be out
quicker than a cat
sees winter.'

They didn't lie,
they filled the car
with noisy bags
oozing with black magic.

A slow crawl home
caught in race day traffic,
a time for praise now
they settled back,
cigarettes on their lips
did a dance.

'She was never any trouble,
God rest her,

not the worst of them,

no way the worst
not by a long shot,

she always had the last word

she did, she did,

she looked so peaceful there laid out

she did, she did,

Like a bone in the bed,

Like a bone in the bed.'

.

Rain and Smart Alec Kids

In Rio de Janeiro
the body wagon comes
to collect the bodies
of children
who die daily
at the wall of goodbyes.

The days
open and close
with grief-stricken parents
on the look out
for death squads
who hate rain
and smart alec kids.

Safe Houses

He sleeps
on couches,
in attics,
in the spare room.

He has learned
the difference between,
attic security
and spare room comfort,
a couch will always be a couch.

He's on the fringe
of favourite bedtime stories,
hush nows it's late,
and promises of
where we'll go next Sunday.

(He's nearly an uncle.)

He hears couples
argue in whispers
and make up without sound.

(These times he dreads.)

He nearly fits in
he's almost secure.

He kisses the floor
when a car pulls up,
an early taxi
or the milkman.

Space Invader

for Louise Hermana

Hey Missus,
you're the poet,
write a poem
about me,

about the time
I lived
in a toilet
for six months,
no shit girlie.

Nothing to whine
home about
but it was dry
and beggars
can't be choosers.

You're the poet,
the one with
the fancy words,

I'm the one
with the toilet—
they call me
the space invader.

A toilet, a toilet
my kingdom
is a toilet—
give us a poem
or piss off missus.

I'm livin'
on twisted pennies
now,
but not for long,

Christmas
is up
round Moon's corner,
and I'll soon
be livin'
off the hog.

I've an uncle
a docker
full card and all
says there's money
in dirty coal yet,

and the coal boat
has a leak,
know what I mean
girlie missus.

Write a poem
about me
about the time
I lived
in a toilet
for six months.

After all
you're the poet
girlie missus
the one with
the fancy words.

Forgotten Prisoner
for Ann Donnellan

Last night
she slipped out
to collect firewood,
it was her turn.

After all
she was eleven now,
an adult since she was six.

Tomorrow,
with the other survivors
she will be fitted with a new limb
a wooden limb,
it will last four years.

In Cambodia only the landmines win.

Voice over the Phone

in memory of Mary Tiernan

Our last meeting,
Sacred Heart School Westport
December 6th 1990.

We both arrived
at the same time,
I didn't know
where to go.

I followed you
up stairs,
and more stairs.

Your voice friendly
your look warm.

Later on
we met again,
we had the tea.

We chatted about
this and that
you said you couldn't keep track
of the new pound coins,
they spent themselves
you said.

We were all
in the staff room
chatting, laughing,

I felt guilty
for having to leave
so soon.

You were down the stairs with me,
this time I led the way.

You said
I was right to go
before the light faded,
you were going to Sligo.

A voice over the phone
told me of your death.
At first I couldn't place you
names and faces danced in my head.

Westport-Sligo
Mary Tiernan, Mary Tiernan.

A voice over the phone said,
she loved life
she was very happy,
yes, that was her
yes, nice clothes
yes, she liked make-up.

In non-stop praise of you
the voice went on,
up stairs and more stairs.

I remembered you well,
your voice friendly,
your look warm.

I remembered you then,
December 6th
slipping off before the light faded.

A voice over the phone said,
you were lovely.

Limits

for Charabanc

There were limits
to what he could take
so he took limits,
sometimes he went
over the limits,

othertimes the limits
went over him,
not in any aggressive way
down the neck way
oil the oesophagus way,

cool and refreshing
on a hot summer's day way;
so he had a problem
he had to watch it.

His mother said it
so did his wife, watch it
the wise ones said, watch it.

But sometimes
when he wasn't looking
limits got him
handcuffed him
forced him into it,
down the neck way
oil the oesophagus way,

when he was
over the limits
nobody wanted him,
he was an unwashed, unwanted,
unwilling, unattractive,
over the limits slob.

Never give a job
to a slob, Bob.
Never give a bob
to a slob.

He never got wise
he only got older,
the limits got higher
the climb got harder.

He reached nowhere
in jigtime,
anywhere in notime.
He had no limits
no fun, no jokes
no-how, no jumpers

only sitters
who sat around with him
and blamed the grass for growing,
the Government
the I.R.A.
the A.B.C.
the I.U.D.
the U.F.O.
the I.T.V.

He was a paid up member
of the
sitters and blamers gang.

After a while
he had no need
to watch it,
limits now looked
for plump ones
half his measure
who still had fight.

He had fought
all his battles
and lost.
He was a lost limit
a limitless loss,

a winner only
when his pockets
were full
and his jokes were new.

Who was he now
at thirty-five—
a limited old man
who hadn't lived;
lingering on street corners,
searching for
shoot-the-breeze friendships
without commitments
or frontiers.

Rat-Like Dogs and Tattooed Men

for Cathy La Farge

In Creepy Crawley
in West Sussex
big men with tattoos
walk rat-like dogs
into pubs.

When the rat-likes
go for the ankle bone
you are told
'Wouldn't touch you.'
Another says,
'He'd lick you to death.'

These big men,
one with his elbow
on his knee,
bellow down the ear
of your friend,

'He's a pisser,
pisses everywhere,
but I'll knock it
out of him,

a few round the head
and he'll sit up.'

You try not to look
at his tattoos
but you can't help it,
they're everywhere,
even on his lips.

'That one's a snake,'
he says,
'an anaconda
could eat elephant eggs
and spit out the shells,
could wrap himself
round the belly of an ass
and strangle it.'

Later, and glad to be home
the whole scene
dances in my head.

I question nothing
but the elephant eggs.

It's Platonic

Platonic my eye,

I yearn
for the fullness
of your tongue
making me
burst forth
pleasure after pleasure
after dark,

soaking all my dreams.

ejacultain

Diction

connotation of sex, but also means occupying

If You Want to
Get Closer to God

A young one like you
shouldn't be left
on your own to wither,
not with the likes
of Kill Cassidy
knocking around.

He'd knock a son
out of you no problem,
no better man,
and he wouldn't even
work up a sweat.

Don't know what
the world's coming to
at all at all.
In Carraroe
they're swopping keys.

God will get
the upper hand yet,
they'll all end up
filling holes in the road
with their sins,
and their Jezebel shoes.

The Claddagh church
is my favourite
there's a lovely one
of the Virgin there
a right beauty,

they say the sculptor
hit ecstasy
before he finished
the five sorrows,

seven hours the ecstasy lasted
down on one knee, mouth open
chisel in the writing home position.

Badly off,
Bad mouth Keogh
said it was no ecstasy
when he saw the bone setter
trotting on his jaw the next day.

Yeah, the Kill Cassidy's
the boy for you,
he'll knock a son alright
as many sons as you like
no better man,

I'm not mad about
the new Cathedral myself
too many frills for my liking,

keep it simple is my motto.
If you really want to get closer to God
Knock Shrine's your man,
no frills, no fuss
stark reality,
plenty of wheelchairs
plenty of buses.

New York

The Korean
who runs a flower shop
in Brooklyn says,

'Every day
people come in here
and steal from me.

They say,
when they are edging out
with my flower basket,

Come on man
my wife just had four babies,
what can I tell you
I look at her
she gets pregnant.

Try taking this from me man
and for your trouble
I'll give you a bullet
in the head.   .

Although
all Koreans love a song,
I never say
Have a nice day
I always say,
Take the flowers.'

H-Block Shuttle

for L. McKeown

We see nothing
from the Inter-Kesh-Shuttle
the H-mobile,
only the people seated
on the other side
(and no one really knows
what side they are on).

Somewhere between H's,
an overdue light bill,
thoughts of a holiday for two
(in anywhere but Gibraltar)
and the one who's doing life,

the H-mobile stops,
we wait for the doors to open
Tic toc, tic toc, tic toc.

Time for a head count.
He counts our heads
on his fingers
for a living,
while the people seated here
count the relatives
they have left,

(some are running
out of uncles).
Some brazen it
with a false laugh,
some stare ahead
forgetting to blink.

A woman whispers
'We're going to the showers,'
others throw Mass card glances
at their shoes
(with them he counts
the back of their heads).

'Hey mister,
what do you do
for a shilling,
a queen's shilling?'

'I count heads
for a living,
my clean living.'

'Do you speak
to the heads
that you count?'

'I'm not paid
to speak to the heads
who don't count.

I'm paid to count
the heads who don't speak.'
'And why
do the heads
that you count
not speak?'

'Outside the dogs bark
to ensure
that the heads
who don't count
that I count
don't speak . . . .'

'And what about
the no-windows scare?'

'No windows are there
to ensure
that the heads
who don't count
that I count
don't see.'

'And what is
it out there
that the heads
who you count
shouldn't see?'

'I count heads
on my fingers
for a living,
for my clean living,
for my queen's shilling.

I get paid
to count heads
who don't count,
not to tell you

what the heads
who don't count
that I count
shouldn't see.'

We see nothing
from the Inter-Kesh-Shuttle,
the H-mobile,
only the people seated
on the other side
(and no one really knows
what side they are on).

His Mother Won't Die

The underwear I have
is older than my last child
and she'll soon be wearing a bra,

and he's down there
every night
throwing pints into himself,
the dirty pig,
and when he falls home
he'll try his hand
at throwing into me,

and his mother won't die
and when she comes over
she says, 'Put more potatoes on it
our Jack has the winter to keep out,

and isn't life easy for you
with your legs spread
before the fire,

and our Jack
lifting wet coal bags
the whole day long
to keep clothes on yer back,

and then you greet him
with that face,
I don't know how he stomachs you.'

Trapped Doctor on Cork
to Galway Bus

He was on the
Connemara run
for years,

twelve pins, twelve bins,
he knew them all.

He grew tired
of the mountains
and the sheep.

He longed
for the sight
of a field of grass,
nothing to write home about,
just a square field
an honest field
level and unpretentious.

He'd still take it
with a cow in it
maybe an old bath
a few rusty gates for a fence,
no sheep or mountains need apply.

He always said
there was a trapped doctor inside him
'One day I'll go back to college'

was his swan song.
Back to Cork
was as far as he got;
it's a long way
depending on how you walk it.

One day
on the Cork to Galway
on the hottest day of the year,
while we sizzled,
a draught fantasizer asked him,
could he open the door please.

He said it was against regulations.

That night
when he made love
to his wife,
he said,

'Gloria love, Gloria,
let on I'm tall.'

The Power of Prayer

I liked the way
my mother
got off her bike
to the side
while the bike
was still moving,
graceful as a bird.

We watched out for her
after Benediction.
It was a game—
who saw her head-scarf first,
I nearly always won.

The day the youngest
drank paraffin oil
we didn't know what to do.

All goofed round the gable end,
we watched, we waited,
head-scarf over the hill.

Knowing there was something wrong
she threw the bike down
and ran.

She cleared fences
with the ailing child,
Mrs Burke gave a spoon of jam,

the child was saved.
Marched indoors
we feared the worst,
our mother knew
what the problem was.

'Not enough prayers
are being said in this house.'

While the paraffin child
bounced in her cot
we prayed and prayed.

We did the Creed,
a blast of the Beatitudes
the black fast was mentioned,
the Confiteor was said
like it was never said before,
Marie Goretti was called
so was Martha,
we climaxed on the Magnificat.
After that it was all personal stuff.

I liked the way
my mother
got off her bike
to the side
while the bike
was still moving,
graceful as a bird.

For good neighbours with jam
for Pope's intentions
for God's holy will
for the something of saints
the forgiveness of sins
for the conversion of Russia
for Doctor Noel Browne
for the lads in the Congo
for everyone in Biafra
for Uncle Andy's crazy bowel
for ingrown toenails
and above all
for the grace of a happy death.

Jackdaw Jaundice

When the geezer
on the bridge
near Heuston Station
asked the nun
for the price
of a cup of tea,

her answer was in
the hooves from hell sounds
she made with her heels.

He replied in winegorian chant,

'Typical jackdaw jaundice,
clip-clopitty-clop
and a black sail away.'

I Want to Make Love
to Kim Basinger

I'm terrified
of hairdressers
who always say
Are you going
to the dance
tonight love?

I always say yes
even though
I'm never going
to the dance
tonight love.

They say the dance
I say the dance
we all say the dance
we say, the dance.

They think
I should be going
to the dance
and what they think goes.

I always
have my hair done
so I can look good
in the bath
in case
Kim Basinger
calls round.

If she takes the trouble
to climb four flights,
the lift isn't there
so it doesn't work,
and if she takes
the further trouble
of five lefts,
two rights
and three straight aheads,
I want to be ready for her.

I never told them this
at the hairdressers,
I always say dance dance,
I'm going to the dance.

It pleases them,
they go from there
they spread the web
cast the nets
they get to the root,
before I know it
I'm on the Persian carpet.

One called Consumpta consumes,
she talks in scrunch and blow dry
kiss curl mousse or gel
bee-hive-jive, French plait
Afro comb all alone.

With her, everyone is my woman;
my woman this, my woman that
my woman with the highlights
my woman with the perm
my woman with the worm.

When consuming Consumpta says
did you just have a baby,
your hair is falling
into your tea.
I always say yes
I start to shout,
I say yes Consumpta yes.

Give her anything
but split ends.
She says,
give me anything
but split ends.

No split ender
ever shifted
the bull of the ball
and we do want
the bull of the ball
don't we
otherwise why bother
getting our hair done
in the first place,
then she says Spanish,

she says Comprendo.
I say yes Consumpta yes.
Once after shouting
over her shoulder
to other, as yet,
less Consuming Consumptas;
Remind me I owe the till three pounds,
she looked me in the eye,
through the mirror,
and said,

hot oil, that's it,
hot oil
is the jigger you need.
Steeped in it
for twenty
you'll come out
a new woman,
you'll taste your tea then
and it won't be wearing a moustache,
mark my words.

And dance, dance
don't talk to me
about dance,
you'll be dancing
that much,
they'll be seeing
sparks off your nipples,

hot oil, that's it

the jigger you need,

hot oil today
the bull of the ball tonight.
Mark my words.

Flight of Pearls

I'm raving
with this flu,
the cough is getting worse
more like a bark every day.

Downstairs
eggshells are crucified
for my benefit
(for tea I get Spam).

The family
are floating
above chair level
(Queen Anne Style).

The youngest
has risen
above the three birds
going up the landing
(Coronation Street Style);
the wild geese.

And someone,
it must be Uncle Someone,
keeps saying
at the top of his voice,
'For Christ's sake
will someone let in
that cursed dog,

I'd do it myself
only I'm up to my eyes
filling out
the census form.'

And the brothers
I forgot to mention
the brothers,
I have seven,
all called Dmitry,
'Ask him,
the one
who wants
to let in the dog
we don't have.'

They say in unison
'Yo, Uncle Nothing,
has immigration
not reached you yet
out there on that limb.'

The Woman Who Lived Here

When she fled
with the children
she left the house
in such a state,

with the bread
gone green mould
and the tea
half drunk in cups.

Kids clothes
sour memories
and echoes of voices loud,

and that smell
of something rotting
decay it was, decay.

That cobwebby smell
that walked up to you
in the hall and said,

'The woman who lived here
pissed fear.'

We were paid
to put a clean face on things
scoop up all interrupted
eggshells.

We were young
we cared little
for something rotting
decay it was, decay.

When she fled
with the children
and left the house
in such a state,

we thought she was dirty.